Wild Strawberries
At 3,000 Feet

Wild Strawberries At 3,000 Feet

poems and stories by

Robert W. Olmsted

This is a publication of the Conservatory Of American Letters, a non-profit Maine corporation.

ISBN 0-89002-242-9

Cover photo by the author

**Northwoods Press
PO Box 88
Thomaston, Maine 04861**

Acknowledgements-

Once Upon A Dream first appeared in **The Magic Ring, (1973)**edited by Joseph McLaughlin

One Eve More, One Less first appeared in *Northern Lights (1969)* edited by Ira Hindman

In The Old Country, A Stroll, Promises To Keep, first appeared in **Shadows On Casseopeia (1976)**

A New Order Of Things first appeared in *Wild Fennel(1977)* edited by Pauline Palmer.

Oleh.   . .Chief first appeared in a different form, in **The Western Virginia Sportsman (1963).**

A special acknowledgement, and thank you, for proof reading and editorial help from Carol Adler.

For Jim

*In the garden of the Gods
There are no buttercups.
Instead there are men.*

Contents

Other books by Robert Olmsted

Northern Lights (1969)
First Christmas Ever (1972)
Shadows On Casseopeia (1976)

Once Upon A Dream

In the cool quiet nether-gloom of the forest
An invisible dream unfolds—
Forms dance about a black-flamed fire
Leaves rustle in a wind not there
Shadows flicker across his face,
Fleeting glimpse, reflected refractions
A white hand tugs gently at the purse
     strings of his soul

Into the magic ring he steps

    All the world is hushed

Now he's there
Now he's not

    But pagan turned to dust.

One Eve More, One Less

Come walk with me by the pond
In the moonlight.
Never mind the bugs, we'll break a
Leafy branch to swish them all away.

Listen. Beyond mosquitoes
Hum you'll hear the frog
Singing to his lady love.
Look quick! See the rings spread
Where the trout rose to take a fly?
Poor fly—lucky trout— one to die,
One to live. God and Socrates only
Know which is better —and perhaps the
Trout swimming in his lair waiting yet
Another bug to fall or hatch.

Let's wander across
The field and back to home.
The children are all sleeping by now.
The night is cool and beckons sleep.
It was an eve of rest, of growing older
Alone together beside the silvered pond.

Journey To Ellsworth

Ellsworth 37.

The arrow pointed right. He eased the big car through the fog onto the right lane. The big engine was loafing at the fog/rain induced 35 mph.

"Save on gas," he said aloud to no one, his brain merely causing the articulation of a coherent thought.

It was a strange day. Early winter, with rain and fog changing the coast road from a beautiful well known route to something else. Something strange and unknown. The bare trees and rocks appeared and disappeared. Oncoming traffic appeared with two boring eyes as it materialized and passed him, sound muffled behind the fog and the tsk-tsk of the wipers, working with barely enough moisture to keep from squeaking. Absent-mindedly, with no conscious thought, he extended his left arm and pulled on the headlight button. A light red light came on over the speedometer, the only touch of color in his grey, black and white world.

The trees slipped by, traffic was light, then none at all for a time. His mind wandered, but he didn't know where. He became a zombie, mesmerized by the road, the fog intermittently clearing so the ghostly trees, growing out of rocks could close in. The road became a tunnel flaring from him.

He did not sleep, nor was he awake. He did not die, nor was he alive. He simply moved through an endless tunnel of fog and rain and trees and rocks. Wisps of clearings cropped up, but they were always small pockets with finite boundaries quite apparant and nearby.

A constant *deja vu* played tricks on his mesmerized mind, and he did not think to try to understand. He was nowhere. He was traveling along going from nowhere to Ellsworth on a road that went nowhere.

I remember you. On the ship. The ship in the fog off the harbour. The ship I could see through fog as though the fog were not there. You were there, standing on the port bow staring straight ahead, no expression. I remember. And before. When I walked behind the hearse with the music making my feet want to dance while my heart wept. My eyes. How they burn in this fog, this god-awful fog of sulpher and smoke. This devil's mist. You were there beside me. We walked through swinging doors across the sawdust and oyster shell floor. We tried to drink our ale, warm and wet. Only it was not ale, but simply the amber fog forced into a glass. We could not drink it, and I was lost forever, walking in a heavy wood. Big trees draped in fog with slanting starlight sparkling through spaces between dead limbs as white as bones. And it was not yet.

Remember when I saw you first? You were beside the door, the wind blew your long hair. We could hear the ocean pounding the rocks. The wind whistled and it was cold. But I felt none of it as fire from your eyes danced and erupted in your face and you erupted in your own flame and I stood looking, not in horror, but in wonder as you became ash and fell to the cobblestone walk and the wind drifted over you and you were gone.

And then the fog horn grew from the sound of your breathing and it rent the fog and the night with a hollowness that came from the very soul of those who died at sea when the wind and the fog make life a fractured gamble without reason and life and non-life were like the horizon which did not exist anyway.

I remembered. You were getting the horse ready for the great race. There were people all around. People with no faces. They made sounds but not words. The dust was heavy and when the horses came around the track the black was out front, straining at the bit, with head low and ears back and a gleam in his eyes as his mane flew and intermingled with the dark, faceless formless man with white teeth shining in the evening sunlight and behind only dust; a huge billowing cloud of sudden earth born into a whirlwind. The other horses were in there somewhere trying to catch the black horse ridden by the black man in the black of night surrounding the finish line. Someone gave you silver. You knew you had won. Thirty pieces of silver glinted in the greyness of the moon blinking through the sudden grey clouds that dropped swirls of snow and

4

fog and mist until the horse was no more.

The road curved and hours passed and he remembered things that never were. Plowing with a wooden plow with three sons pulling on the rope. The ground was cold and black and as the shallow furrow formed, fog rose from the earth and his sons disappeared as the plowed ground widened and they walked in their own fog. There was nothing. Nothing but the next step and the grip of the plow and the fog. Always the fog. Now it was filled with sound, now it was silent. Silence shattered by a scream, then the fog reddened and the scream ended and the moment stopped.

You were with me. Again. As before and before and even to the time when there was no before. You were with me. Can't you remember? Surely when you stand in the fog with the sea crashing at your feet you remember. Or when you are on the sea, and the mist and the snow grow heavy.

Yes, you remember.

Fragments and flakes we call dreams and memories. Other times, other places, other planes, other realities. Other.

There was a fire once, a great burning in the sky. We did not know why, but we were there. You and I. There in the inferno in the sky, and when it stopped there was fog again. Always the fog and the tunnel emanating from you, a tunnel of infinite direction and depth when you are the center, and light, even was bent to your being. We could not understand, or even understand that we could not understand. We simply are and were, and were yet again and the light is soft now and there is a mewing sound of tenderness which ruptures the fog, and there is color now, and light and movement and all that there is is motion and noise and light and color and hardness and softness and a quivering cry that is beyond the rim of the fog and we built a wall to hold it out and a roof to spare our heads and we were awhile in gladness. But the wall was feeble and could not hold the fog and the mist without and it collapsed and we each again stand alone, light emanating from us as the center we could not see.

A sharp form filled the void and I was on board. Sounds reverberated and whined and I rose with motion so fast that blood drained from my eyes and I could not see. When we stopped the earth was far below, spinning in the mist of clouds and whatever else fills the space. It glowed like a luminescent dial of a grand-father clock, or like a harvest moon that rises over a foggy corn-field and quivers on a windless night when only the darkness rustles the leaves as dark tries to escape the blood red glare of the moon.

Like that! But no cornfield, no mountain here. Nothing. Just the earth spinning in an endless mist of fog and ice and darkness. There is no sun, just cold-blooded red luminescence in the night of grey fog. And you are here.

With me, of me, but separate you and me and the engine of the empty care droned onward until we crossed the green bridge hanging from green ropes that hang down from the sky. The green fog and diffused light falls on the green water that sparkles invisible below.

There is no one here. I am alone. I am lost. I have returned to the place of Romeo and Juliet, but it is not the same anymore.

Still the engine drones and I do not sleep. There are sounds I can not hear, but they move the fog and I see them, or the path they take at least. I can see him now. A great buck standing on the dock. His antlers are like whitened trees and the fog stands back from him. He is there in sharp profile. He and the sailing ship below him the only things of form and substance in this grey world of green fog where sounds are seen but not heard.

"Why me?" He did not know, but turned to the right.

Ellsworth 19.

Ellsworth 18.

It is three hours now since he started. He does not know where he has been or why it has taken three hours to traverse nineteen miles. He did not stop. He remembered nothing. The old car purrs along, gas gauge below empty. It is raining harder and the fog has cleared. It is now mostly clear. He passes a lake, swollen to overflow its black cold waters up and around trees along its shore. There are birches here. Starkly white against the black lake. The rocks are grey, like the fog that is held back by the rain, but is there, waiting.

"Where the hell have I been?" He speaks aloud to no one as he looks at his watch, then his gas gauge.

No one answers as he pulls in for gas.

"Five dollars' worth," he says to the man who comes out in the rain. He goes into the store and drinks a coke. He pays but does not speak, though amenities are offered.

Even here the people seem strange. Like mannequins with voice and emotion. Hollow men.

"Thanks," he says to the male mannequin that moves through life but is not part of it.

"What the hell is happening to me? Where've I been?" he says aloud to no one.

"You have been with me."

He was not surprised to hear it and knew before he turned his head to look at her exactly what she would look like.

"Who are you?"

"Don't you know?"

He did not answer at once. A part of him knew. The part which could not articulate thoughts knew, the part which could, did not.

"No."

"You know. You simply choose not to remember now. You will be reminded."

"How?"

"See how the fog rolls in ahead. We enter it soon and we will return. We will be together again, as we have always been together."

"I don't understand any of this. Am I going mad? Have I died? Is this a time warp?"

"The answer to any of those things is probably beyond our conscious understanding. We are, to use words that very nearly describe it but fall far short, involved."

"Involved in what?"

Perhaps the simplest word is. . . in God."

"What's simple about that? Ideas of God are so complex I can not even believe."

"You are right. *God* is a poor explanation. Maybe you are involved with more life than you've ever understood before."

He didn't speak for a long time. He only drove through the fog.

"What is your name?"

"You have just thought it."

He hesitated --"Amanda?"

"You remembered."

"I don't know what I remember, I have not yet looked at you. You can not be real. But I know what you look like."

"Look at me."

It was a command, not a suggestion.

She was there.

"Touch me."

She was there.

"But you are not there. My mind plays games as the three hours I think it took me to drive nineteen miles. My mind plays tricks. The mind is a powerful thing."

"Yes, I know. It can make a heaven out of hell. I've read Milton too."

"But it can."

"Of course it can not," Amanda said; then added: "It can't make anything of nothing. It can see, with varying degrees of clarity that which is. I have been with you always. You have always been with me."

"Are you *death*?" He asked, his voice almost choking.

"I am life."

"Why do I know you as Amanda?"

"Let me show you." The fog rolled heavy, even permeating the inside of the car until even Amanda was not clear. But her presence, her voice, her earth-rich odor were very clear.

He slowed the car and pulled off onto a *Scenic-Turnout-500-feet-ahead.*

There was no scene to view, only fog. Her hand was warm in his.

"Follow me."

He followed her through the woods and up a hill. Near the top of the hill a strangeness overtook him and he knew things were not as he understood them.

"What now?" he asked.

Amanda answered in words he did not know.

"Ud ek nahr."

"What?"

"Ud ek nahr."

"You'll have to speak English."

She looked at him, her eyes deep and bottomless. She did not speak. She held her fingers to her lips and turned. He followed.

There seemed to be a bit of a trail. They were walking along the edge of a hill. The woods gave way to brush, the brush to grass, tall wet grass. The fog was wispy here, not the solid fog of the highway. The afternoon had become dusk.

They turned the hill and the campfire was glowing. There were others there. Not mannequins, but live beings. They looked like people but they were more than that. They were people with other dimensions, other understandings. They chattered in a strange tongue, as Amanda had spoken.

"What are they saying?"

Amanda stopped and turned. She kissed him. Her lips were of fire and salt and the kiss aroused him intently. When their lips parted he spoke her tongue. He understood. Not the words, not the thoughts. They were more than thought, they were reality. They were LASER. That is, Life Amplified with Stimulated Emmissions of Remembering. Whatever power life was before LASER, there was more now. Life with such power that death even had no control. Death could not enter and neither heaven nor hell could have a claim.

"Where are we?"

"We are here."

"Where is *here*, in relation to Rt. 1 in Maine?"

"We are many years from there."

"And these people?"

"Just people, mostly. Struggling for survival as man has always."

"How did we get here?"

"I can not explain the process. It is LASER."

"Is that like a time-warp?"

She laughed. "If that will explain it to you, let it be that. It is, perhaps as good as any other term we might discover."

"Where are we then?"

"Come." She led him around the fire and into the night. They walked together through an open forest, across a small brook to the edge of the field. There in the field were giant stones on edge, in a circle. Shadows moved among the stones.

"Stonehenge." He could not believe it. His voice broke as a panic began to swell in his head. "It is not real. You are not real.

This can not be.''

"Be at ease. All things are not only possible, all things are. Do not try to understand it. Simply accept it. Enjoy it. Relax and let the earth turn beneath you. There is no reason for fear. The unknown is not unknown at all, just not yet realized. Besides, we have been here before, you just do not remember.''

He looked at her. She was not as his wife, but as he looked into her eyes he saw the familiar, the comfortable. There was recognition.

"You are. . .''

"Of course I am. Did I not say we have been together always, even before there was a beginning?''

"But —?''

"Don't try it. The conscious and the finite part of you can not make the bridge.''

"You are a witch.''

"Ah, a favorite term of the ignorant and fearful. Like *time warp,* use it if it helps.''

"Then we are druids?''

"That is a term your current life group uses for us. We are subjects of the *Ancient Ones,* the oldest gods, those forces which created even God. We use the temple to measure and trace our trek through time and universe. We use it to pray and to call upon those *Ancient Ones.* Those powers of darkness and light and wind and fire. Those creative forces.''

"I thought they were forces of evil and destruction.''

"Even evil and destruction have to be created. But evil is simply a misunderstanding of what is. As is good. The *Old Ones* do not know the terms *evil* and *good,* only purpose and movement.

"Then what is our purpose?''

"Who do you imagine to be the most intelligent, wisest person who has ever lived?'' she asked, as she started off toward the temple.

He walked with her in thought, silent for many strides; the temple drew nearer.

"Perhaps DaVinci, or Jonathan Swift.''

"Jonathan? He is here.''

"Here? But Swift was long after the druids.''

10

She laughed, "And so are you, and I. But we are here. Would you like to meet him?"

"I guess so, but does he too speak the strange tongue?"

"Of course, even as you and I. We are speaking that *strange* tongue. You don't seem to be having any problem."

"I'm speaking English."

"English is a fine name for it. But I assure you, people from the other side of your time warp would not be able to understand a word, even as you could not when first we arrived."

He did not speak again until they reached the temple. The shadows and forms they'd seen from the edge of the field were now people. All dressed in white robes, all moving about, to and from, here and there, seemingly aimlessly and without purpose. Amanda walked to a group of four talking forms. One looked up. separated from the others and walked with Amanda towards him.

"I am flattered that you imagine me one of the wisest persons who has ever lived. Where did you get such a thought?" The man looked at him carefully. He stared long into his eyes, then "Have we met before?"

"No. That is, we couldn't have." He hesitated, realizing. "Well, maybe. I don't remember."

"I think I do," he said.

"He's just in from the other side. he is quite confused by everything," Amanda explained.

"To be sure," Jonathan said, kindly. "How can I help you?"

"I don't know. I seem lost, disjoint. Nothing is as my remembered life experience says it should be."

"He learns fast. He is already qualifying statements. Good awareness. I like that. He'll do well." Jonathan nodded approvingly to Amanda.

"He has ever done well. His conscious mind wants to know of purpose, meaning."

"To what?" Jonathan asked him.

"I don't know. I'm confused. To life I guess."

"And what do you imagine is the purpose of life?"

"I have no idea. I have read and read and talked with others. They often state reasons, purposes. But none of them makes sense or stands up under the simplest question. I am with Omar, the tent maker-

> *Myself when young did eagerly frequent*
> *Doctor and Saint, and hear great argument*
> *About it and about: But evermore*
> *Came out be the same door as in I went.*

—I simply have no idea.''

''And you think I do?''

''Well, no. That is, I never thought about it. Amanda simply asked me who I imagined to be the wisest person who ever lived. I suggested you, or DaVinci.''

''And you quote Omar.''

''That quatrain just sort of popped in.''

''Of course, in a lineal time frame it is not yet written.''

''But you still know it?''

''Of course, doesn't everyone?''

''No. Everyone I know does not know it. Few do.''

''That is sad. You in your present sojurn live in an ignorant age. An age when our race is caught up in some of the tiny, insignificant secrets of technology. Technology is more important, in your eyes, than is man. Anything that your tiny technology can not explain is relegated to either myth, the occult, or the supernatural. Come, let us sit and talk some more.''

''Am I dead?'' He realized the word was wrong and felt stupid.

''No. Not in any sense, not even to your own age.''

''Will I get back home?''

''Of course. Unless you do something foolish like drive into a truck in the fog.'' He laughed.

''How do you know it is foggy?''

''It is always foggy when we get visitors. The fog seems to condition the mind to acceptance; though most, while they accept, rarely realize. Nor can they articulate it.''

''You mean this happens often?''

''Oh yes. We are all visitors here. Leonardo has come. So too Omar. Many of the men and women of the arts, many technologists too. Mostly we get ordinary people, with no reputation at all, in any age. We are all visitors. No one is ever unwelcome. We talk, we listen, we learn, and in turn, we teach.''

"Then you do know the purpose of life?"

"Nay. Not I. If that is your quest it will likely go un-answered."

"Then is there a reason for my being here? For this, this, uh. . ."

"Experience." Amanda offered the word.

"To be sure."

"What is it?"

"I don't know."

"Who does know?"

"Only you."

"Me? I don't know. I was just driving to Ellsworth to see a man about a computer and suddenly there was Amanda."

"Were you surprised or afraid when you saw her?"

"No." The answer came quickly, matter-of-factly. He had not been surprised or afraid and had known instantly what she looked like before he turned to look at her.

"And what thoughts did you have? Before she joined you?"

"I don't know. No thoughts. Nothing. The world seemed strange. The fog was moving about making things seem unreal. At one point I thought I'd been driving forever. It seemed as though it took many hours to travel only nineteen miles. But I wasn't thinking about anything, at least not coherently. I seemed to be moving in and out of the present."

"Always to the past?"

"No, I don't think so. But I'm not sure. Neither past nor present nor future had much substance."

"You are approaching something called *truth*. Where did you find him, Amanda?"

"He wrote about it once, in a poem. At an early potato harvest in Scotland, with me."

"In what time frame?"

"1826"

"I don't know that that helps much," Jonathan said. Then, "You write of strange things, do you not?"

"Well, they don't seem strange to me. But others seem to think them strange sometimes."

"I see. How do you get your information?"

"What information? I don't write much informational stuff

anymore.''

"Why not?''

"I don't know. It just seems to be a waste of time.''

"How's that?''

"Well, you know. I don't *know* anything. Any information I have is based on what I have read or done. I've not done anything unusual, nothing original.''

"You write.''

"Yes, but not based on information.''

"What would you call it?''

"I don't know.''

"Is it inspiration?''

"I don't think so.''

"Insight?''

"Maybe. But that doesn't seem right either.''

"Is the purpose of life a haunting question to you?''

"Sort of. I don't know if I think life has a purpose or not. But compared to death it seems purposeful.''

"That's from an inadequate understanding of death. After all, by your calendar, I've been dead for centuries. Do I seem dead to you? Does Amanda?''

"But in death, realization ceases. It hurts when one you love is no longer with you. I mean, even if the dead continue, realization continues: the ones left alive no longer have the realization of the one dead.''

"That is sometimes true. That is why we invent religion and ritual. The ritual puts substance to that which seems to have no substance.''

"Let me suggest something," Amanda said. "Suppose one you loved took a long trip, went away for three years or so. Would that be as bad as a death?''

"Maybe it could be, but not usually, I guess.''

"That is death. If your son goes into the foreign service for three years, is that not worse than death? In the foreign service you will not see him for three years. In death you might not see him for a longer period, or a lesser. Perhaps only minutes later, when, with your own death, you join him.''

"But would I know him and he me?''

"Do you know me?" Amanda asked.

He did know her. He did not understand how she could be here and in Rockland at the same time. A sudden shattering thought hit him.

"My god, is Barba. . ."

"She is fine. Everything on the other side is as you left it."

He had a sudden longing to go home. To return to the world he could not understand, but which seemed clearer than this one.

"Can I go now?"

Jonathan rose and extended his hand. "Of course you can go. But now that you've learned the way, you must come again."

"Have I learned the way? What did I do?"

"You sought us. You remembered. You allowed the mind to leave the narrow confines of self and now."

"That's all?"

"Probably. It is different for each of us who finds a way here."

"Do all find their way here?"

"Few, actually."

"And the rest?"

"They go other places, other times. There are many. Many simply wander as aimlessly as in the life journey."

This was heavy and his mind was unwilling to hear more.

"Thank you for talking to me. I may indeed try to come again. Will you be here?"

"Can't say," Jonathan said.

He looked at Amanda.

"I am with you always."

Ellsworth 3.

There was a girl hitchhiking. She looked familiar. She appeared suddenly in the fog. Dark hair hanging straight, dark eyes.

He drove by.

"Can't trust anybody," he said to no one.

A few minutes later he pulled into *Radio Shack* at the **Maine Coast Mall.**

"How're you doing, Bill?" The salesman said, all smiles, hand extended.

He ignored the hand and thought of t.s. elliot's *The Hollow Men,* and then —

     Shanti   *Shanti*   *Shanti*

In The Old Country

Once in the old country when
  I was a peasant
  trying to live on blighted potatoes
  we held a party on the heath.
It was cold and windy, rain
  like ice made us cold.
But the fire was cheery and we danced
  and sang late into the night.
Burning all the brush and stubble
  dancing as though possessed, we laughed
  and sang the night to rest.
Morning found us beneath the
  hill wrapped together against the
  chill rain whipping us.
We were drunk with wine, with
  song and dance and love.
When I was there with you I did dream
  ahead and saw myself warm
  and sheltered and sober and
  protected from all that was bad and
  cruel and lost to all that was
  free.

My youth went and I became a
  man of the future, wrapped in comfort
  and wealth, I could not remember the
  empty hills of a summer's labor,
  nor joys of dancing all night in an early
  autumn rain on the heath
  before a fire where
  witches even may have danced
  and sang their chants.

From life to death I saw
  myself going and I woke my love

and told her to drink the wine and
love me again and live free and
wild and happy, for what is coming
is not so fine.

And she drank the wine and
   pulled me to her and we made
   love again in the wet and cold
   dew of early morning with the mist
   of the heath rising from us and
   from the heather we lay deep among.

Had I been able to see myself
   and had I the power to say
   "hold" I'd have begged, this is it.
I'll go no farther, stop here
   and I'll stay.

But I had no such power
   and the damp drizzle turned to winter
   cold when even the young
   and the wild and the free
   stayed locked inside beside the
   hearth while winter raged.

We waited for springtime, but
   it was slow in coming and when it
   did we were old and it would
   take another summer of blighted
   labor before we could dance again
   and be young again on an autumn heath
   with cold drizzle and rain spilling
   from a hostile sky.

Me And My Shadow

A shadow walked through my room
I was awake.
The shadow thought I slept and did
But dream it into being.

But no.
I was there and saw this
Shadow that did appear.
I wanted to speak to it, but my
Jaws were locked.

Finally
I willed it my way.
Willed it to turn and say

You can not sleep
You must be dead.

My shadow went away.

A New Order Of Things

He looked at his pay check. He cursed.

The office, the boss, the president. He had received only 50 percent of what he had earned. He wanted to scream, to beat someone over the head. But how would that help.

A leaf fluttered in the early autumn wind. Just an early autum n leaf fluttering downward, gently golden. It fell where a man stood.

"Hello," he said, as he approached.

"You look tired."

"Yea." The man had fallen in beside him.

"Why are you so tired?"

"I'm not so tired as angry."

"Why?"

"It is just the way things are. I'm tired of being controlled by the rich, by the poor, by the government. I hate losing 50 percent of my pay check each week while the fat cats in Washington get fatter. I'm mad. I'm also helpless to do anything, and that makes me madder."

"I understand. I think I can show you something you would be interested in."

"What?" then —"forget it. I don't care."

"Oh, no. You care. You care very much, believe me. You care or you wouldn't be angry. You're on your way home?"

"Yea. I live a few blocks up the road. Say, who are you?"

"Call me Nathan. I'm just an itenerant philosopher. Just a rover, a student of human nature."

"Oh—"

"I wwatched you walk out of the building and thought that you were upset. I was curious, thought perhaps I could talk with you, cheer you up a bit."

"I'm just tired and pissed off becuase I have to support all of the Washington corruption. Me. John P. Littleman."

"Is that your name?"

"No. Name's George."

"Well George, I think I can show you something that would interest you."

"Like what?"

"Well, it's a new order of things. Beauty like you've never seen before. It's just outside town. It truly is a new order of things."

"What are you, a real estate salesman?"

"I have nothing to sell."

"Then what?"

"Description is difficult. But here's my car and the distance is not great." He looked at George steadily as he held the door open.

"I don't know why, but okay. So long as I'll be ready for dinner within an hour—"

"Oh, no problem. You'll be ready long before then."

"Then it isn't far?"

"Not at all."

They drove a short distance into the country. George was curious about the man whose voice was soft but had the cold quality of an icepick grating into his mind. There was little said, little time for thought, as the car slowly came to a stop beside a section of early autumn wood. A wide trail led down and away from town, the place was almost unfamiliar. Or perhaps only vaguely familiar, though he knew he must have been there before. Perhaps it was the rose-colored twilight on the early golden leaves.

"Come. It is just down the trail a short walk."

"Yea? What's short?"

"A couple of hundred yards or so. Or as the ancients used to say, a stadia or so."

"What's a stadia?"

"An old measurement. Perhaps 200 yards."

"What am I to look for on this trail?"

"As I promised. It is a new order of things."

"That's vague—Look! A deer."

The trail curved to the left, and standing at the edge was a deer. As George watched her, her tongue flicked out and caught a large toad. Its struggles were useless, as the tongue simply retracted into the mouth of the deer, taking the toad with it. The deer lifted its head and watched them approach, doe-eyed, licking her lips absently with the long raspy tongue.

20

George stopped, but Nathan walked on. George wanted to speak, but Nathan looked at George and put his finger to his lips. George followed. The deer did not move until they walked by her; then, at 20 feet, she followed.

This must be his pet, George thought. But Nathan made no sign of recognition. It was dark in the forest, yet George could see everything in a soft evanescent glow. The deer followed.

"Here—" Nathan pointed.

"There was a small pond of rainwater beside the trail.

"What?"

"To see and understand you have to lie down and look very closely. Go ahead. It is beautiful. Well worth it."

George sighed, thinking perhaps of humoring his hamrless host. He stretched out on the edge of the trail and looked at the pond. In miniature, close up. The moss, the gentle light, the reflection in the rose reflecting water, the leaves, a blade of grass bent over the far shore, another broken at right angles, a tiny circle where something under the surface, something very tiny, moved against the film, all made a beautiful world in miniature. New, unseen, pure. As he stared, he heard Nathan's voice, as though from another world, a thin echo.

"Is it not truly beautiful?"

"Yes. It is. I see it."

"Look more closely."

"Yes. I am."

"Is it not a new order of things? Is it not truly a new order?"

"Yes. I agree. It really is."

Then George screamed as Nathan stepped aside and the deer began calmly to devour George.

Promises To Keep

We meet again
To love again
As we loved before in some dim past
when milkmaids sat on three legged
stools and cowherds leered at shapely
thighs beneath tight stretched ginghams.

Love me, for
We are eternity.

Remember how I chased you through the meadow?
In the tall grass by the stream
with the evening sun redding the sky?
You allowed yourself to be caught.
Your breath was warm with the
freshness of milk, your breasts rose and fell
as you recovered from the race
you never meant to win.
Your lips told of yearning
And we met,
empty souls each to be filled.

We made love as the night settled over us.
Distant thunder promised rain.
We promised to love again
to outwit death
to outwait him.

We keep a promise of two centuries.
As the night gives way to morning,
passion to content
let us promise again
to love again.

(with apologies to Don Marquis)

you know boss
its been a long time since
i could kick up my heels and have
fun

once i was a man maybe
more than once im never quite
certain and a free verse poet
it was fun then for 68 years
i was entrapped in the shell
of a cockroach

dont get me wrong now
im not knocking cockroaches
in the universal order of things
cockroaches have a spot
but it is a rather confining form
oh we had our games and our fun
but
well take sex for instance
dry boss
and brittle
better then nothing to be sure
but hardly the sort of thing
to set ones soul in ecstasy

as a cockroach i remembered sex
as being better when i was human

but now now i know why francois villon
used to chant i am a cat of the devil i am
but now as a tomcat
i cant remember what sex was like
when i was human
there not only seems a lot more of it now
but no one expects you to sign papers or
hear a sermon before you indulge

and fidelity feline fidelity
it means something else boss
im not sure i know what

i must say relative to sex at least
this most recent transmigration may be a step
up even from the time i was a poet

oops mehitabel is calling
yea boss i know im under the little red puss'
thumb
i admit it
you know why mehitabel stays an alley cat boss
she told me
because she likes it
shes been cleopatra   she says that was nice
and a few other famous and infamous broads
but the last time she reincarnated she turned down
a human baby girl of very well off parents
chose to wait for a fancy cats coat
to re enter

she made it boss she made it
shes fancy
she really enjoys being a cat
i do too boss
i do too
archy

Wild Strawberries At 3,000 Feet

I picked them there
with winter a cruel memory
and summer an inverted time warp
extending backward and outward into
realms of floating sunshine and silent
whispers of breezes on grasses and the
berries, tiny rich, deep in the green
of the Meadows Of Dan and/or the Scotland
Highlands of 1977/1377 and
the berries and the summer and me
fill the basket with eternity.

Summer holds and time cannot stand still
for it can not exist.

We lay on our backs, close against the earth
and look down forever into the blue.
We are eternity, intermingling pasts
in confusion as we live the
warm and sweet smell
of summer earth and sky
as the earth holds us,
safe above nothingness
running blue below.

We have waited, and it did not move.
The earth is still and only we exist,
We, the man, the boy, the mountain, the
basket of red life and the void
below. We are still,
and with wild strawberries, are forever.

A Stroll

I walk and remember when I
was a Spaniard near Barcelona.
It was 1282.

I was poor, unkempt, lonely.
I worked the soil with a wooden hoe.

Now I am not unkempt.

I walk on,
A river makes me think of an aqueduct I labored on
to bring fresh water to the rich,
the citizens.
I drank only wine, our water stank.
It was unclean.

I walk by the cemetery and stand beside
the weathered stone of my father.

I remember great pyramid-tombs.
The priests made the great stones move
of themselves, but thousands of us
labored to place them while the
priests held them motionless
in the hot afternoon sun, waiting for
directions of the foreman.

I remember.
Well I remember.
I was buried in a cloth.
I died building a tomb for god.

And before?

A strange world I can not see.
It was not this world.

Oleh. . . Chief! Grandfather!

> *Unhousled, disappointed, unanel'd*
> *No reckoning made, but sent to my account*
> *with all my imperfections on my head.*
>
> ***Hamlet,*** I, V 77-79

He had hunted that valley for years. He'd almost hoped he'd die there some year, alone, more than ten miles from the nearest trail. The valley with its small brook murmuring through, high in the Maine mountains, was the only place on the face of the earth that he could go and be alone. He went every year, in early November; he spent from one week to two, hunting deer. It wasn't good hunting. He always managed to get a deer, but he could have gotten a better one close to home. The mountain deer seemed smaller, faster, more afraid. He seldom took home trophies. There had been a time fifty years ago when he'd taken four big ones right in a row, all descendents of the biggest buck he had ever seen, the one too big, even for a young man, to kill.

Once or twice he'd taken others with him into the high country, but they'd never wanted to make the trip again. Better trophies were easier had in the lower hills, close to roads. A walk of only a couple of hundred yards would put venison on the Thanksgiving table.

Even his own son wouldn't go back. That had hurt. It was the legacy of his own dying nation denied. He'd gone three times, when he was fourteen, fifteen and sixteen. When he was seventeen he'd said, "What do you want to go way up there for? I can get a better deer right around here."

"Not better. Tamer. Anyone can."

"Then why drag yourself up and over a 3,000 foot mountain to get a small deer? It doesn't make sense."

It hurt, a little. He enjoyed the solitude, had to have it. But the years when he had taken one man, or boy, with him were good. They didn't destroy the solitude, and the silent company of a man watching a campfire on an Indian Summer night was a greater joy than watching it alone.

He wondered this year if it would be his last. He wondered every year, lately. He was getting old, it now took him eight or ten hours to hike in over the ridge. He was tough and hardened, but he was seventy-some. His wife, sons, and friends all said he shouldn't go again. But he went. Alone.

This year had been no different. He had crossed the ridge three hours ago and sat resting beside the little brook. It wasn't much more than a foot wide, but it was full of delicious little trout. His mouth watered as he contemplated them.

He could see that his cache had weathered well. In the past ten years or so he had been leaving things up here. In five-gallon tins with tops, carefully sealed and hung thirty feet up in an old pine beside the stream. In them he'd find many things that made his visit more comfortable. Tarps, tools, axe, lantern and fuel, cooking utensils, extra blankets, extra bullets he'd never needed but which he replaced each year, a 22 revolver, and a pair of folding snow shoes he'd also never needed. The snowshoes were made for him by his old friend, Joe Cloud. Joe made snowshoes to sell to the tourists in the summer, and then good snowshoes for the residents. They were expensive, but the tourist didn't need quality, he'd never use them, and the local people didn't need fancy because they'd never look at them. Joe charged them all the same, both were satisfied, both got their money's worth. Joe Cloud made enough snowshoes to live on between January and May each year. The rest of the year he fished and hunted and laughed at others who worked too much. Joe might do a little guiding if you caught him in a good mood, but other work he'd none of.

"Damn fool white man work too hard, fish too little. He have it backward." Joe Cloud's Indian diction occured in exact proportion to the person he spoke to. For summer people, he was Indian. To anyone else he was Maine, down East. English no different from what any white man spoke. He'd been raised as a white man, educated in the white public schools, even spent a couple of years at Orono. He was Indian only for the tourists. Cloud had built him a special pair of webs with leather hinges that folded to fit the cans. He greased the leather every year and sealed the can with wax he melted so they'd stay air tight. The snowshoes had never been needed. He'd been caught in a couple of snows, but they'd been small ones, and usually melted before he needed shoes. Once, before he'd had them, he'd needed them.

The old man that rested beside the stream was far different from the young man who'd chased a huge buck up here nearly fifty years ago. He was wiser now, but that was little consolation to his heaving lungs and aching legs. Making camp was a chore. He carefully lowered his several tins and checked them for damage. He opened them and emptied their contents before he sprayed all the spots where paint had chipped off. The spray can of blue enamel packed up every year, and taken home again, still half full. No rust. He feared rust, the slow burning of that which wouldn't burn any other way than slowly, without heat. A decay of the hard, solid, undecayable.

Setting up camp was routine and automatic even if it did take longer; he was resting before his campfire before dark. In the dusk he looked at the camp and was pleased. He was at home again. It had been one year and one day since he'd set up camp here. It was good to be home. Heaven, if it existed at all, must be like this. The happy hunting grounds of his father, his, for seven to fourteen days, by license of the state, which cost a couple hours' wage. A couple hours' wage of a year's work, minus these days and a few others he'd steal to fish in. Only now he didn't work for wages. His little, too little, social security check came every month, and he did some guiding for fishermen in the summer. His son contributed a little and kept taxes and insurance on the house paid. They got on well, he and the woman that had owned his house for forty years.

She'd come with him once, the first year they were married. It was the only year he had not gotten a deer up here. He had felt uncomfortable with her in the valley. She claimed to like it, to really enjoy it, but she never came again. The next year their son was three months old. The following year he had measles, then there was something else, then he was in school, and she was never able to make the trip again. This was wilderness only for man, and it seemed, only for one man.

As he sat musing by the campfire, he felt the first touch of fatigue. An old man on a cool night waiting for the snow, being whispered to by tall pines. Firelight faceflecked on the dignity of a dying nation now asleep, dreaming perhaps of days when young men chased old bucks and young women.

He awoke sometime before dawn, cold. A heavy frost silvered the forest. His fire was just embers, but he stirred it quickly, and gnarled old hands put gnarled old twigs on the embers. Fire and warmth came quickly, and the hunter began to acquire all the excitement of the hunt. He knew exactly where he would go. He knew he would see deer. He also knew he would not shoot. Not for a week. He had to have that much time to breathe the mill stench from his body, to cleanse his blood, to empty his soul and to ease his spirit from the turmoil of the world he lived in but could not understand. He needed a few days to revert to the wilds that had nurtured his people. Then he needed a few more days to enjoy the reunion. He would shoot no deer this week. Unless —maybe not even then— it was a trophy bigger than the ones he already owned which were bigger than any others he had ever seen. He'd seen one bigger deer, the father of the ones he'd killed, he believed. It had simply been too magnificent to kill. No, there'd be no deer hanging before Monday.

The eastern ridge began to fade light as he finished his fried eggs and bacon. He sat with his back to a log and drank hot black coffee as he watched the dawn come and the night go. He'd watched it before, but still held it in awe. The mystery of the phoenix without the need for ashes. Where was the phoenix of his people? Ashes were everywhere. Perhaps theirs was a cuckoo phoenix and could only rise from borrowed ashes.

He stood just west of the game trail where it crossed the ridge and where for almost forty years he had started the season. He'd always seen deer. Always the same ones, it seemed. Today was no different. He hadn't been settled ten minutes when he heard the brittle underbrush crackle with the light steps of the whitetail. There were four of them: one big doe, two of last year's fawns and the ageless, timeless forkhorn. The hunter could not be sure of the time. He was suspended in the experiences of his past and the realities of his present.

He watched the procession browse past in the amber chill of the early morning. He knew he'd see no more deer, but he was comfortable with the pine air cleaning his lungs, fresh oxygen feeding his tired arteries, clearing the pollutants of civilization from his body. An old man learns patience, learns to appreciate little things, like the snow birds that flitted about, and the day coming with certain speed, unheeded, unaided, peaceful. He sat till almost noon, then headed down the ridge toward camp. When he was younger, he shot the gray squirrel that always worked around his stand. Now he only wanted to watch the squirrel, to enjoy its freedom; he did not want to eat it. He wanted to eat trout. Much better now than at any other time. They were fatter, richer, and easier to catch, and perhaps better because the state, that belonged to his people when boundaries were not needed, said he could not catch them at this time of year. It pleased him to catch what he needed. Clean food, doing to his body what clean air did to his spirit. Catching, cleaning and wrapping the extra trout in clean moss was ritualistic. They had to be handled with a certain reverence, and the aesthetic element of design and placement had to be acknowledged. But the hunter didn't know this; he simply did what he wanted to do. If you had told him he was eating his brother when he ate the trout, it might not even have evinced a smile.

The week passed like many others, except that he grew tired quicker, stayed on stands after he should have moved, waiting, waiting for the tiredness to leave him. He saw plenty of deer. He knew the deer so well he was almost one of them, he knew where they bedded, when they arose and in which direction they'd likely go when they began their evening browse. Seeing deer, even a nice eight point buck, was no problem. Time was the problem.

Towards the end of the first week, he began to feel his spirit lift. The cleansing was removing the ballast from his soul, freeing it to the mountain breezes, heavy laden with the scent of fall, and lately, the smell of snow. He thought of Cloud's snowshoes. This year he'd need them.

When he awoke the morning of the eighth day, it was snowing. Cold blowing white flakes, tiny and significantly insignificant. There was no morning. The gray whirling night simply changed to gray whirling day. The hunter, his webs strapped to his back, was on the trail at what would have been dawn had there been a dawn. He welcomed the snow. It was the final purifying agent his spirit needed. Somewhere in the dim remembrance of his mind he saw, without knowing, the symbolic purity of the snow. He even hoped he would be snowed in, would have to stay all winter. It couldn't happen. He had good webs, he was strong, and he could walk out over many feet of snow with little problem. Still, his subconscious remembered.

The hunter sat in the silent snow, waiting. There were three inches of silence on the forest floor. He waited. The forest was hushed, expectant, almost sinister. The old hunter suddenly knew what he was waiting for. As suddenly as he knew, the buck appeared, moving slowly, his massive antlers held high. A big non-typical rack bigger than any he'd ever seen, bigger than any deer that had ever walked these forests. The hunter was unable to move. He p r o b -
ably never thought to shoot, awed as he was by the wildness and nobility of the buck. He felt the fatigue again in his chest and the buck started fading. Not running, just walking, fading, step by step into the nothingness of the gray snow. Not even walking out of sight, fading back into the wilderness it never left. Its disappearance left the woods empty except for the falling, swirling, silent snow.

Reflected Immortality

Come, let's walk to the spring
simmering warm
in icy air.
Warm enough to flow from source
several rods before
it chills to ice.
Warm enough to fog
the branches and twigs,
specters of ghostly white.

Look into the water,
see the sky reflected above
pebbles and sticks.
A world where
Indians drank hundreds of years ago,
wild things before that.

Our children will drink here
and know us as we know the
Indians and wild things.

The Woodchuck

We lay in the tall sweet-smelling grass
with colors of violet and gold —fresh
tasting, aromatic as the white scudding sails
above. Half-grown green
leaves wavered in the breeze, almost black
against blue. A cloud of bothersome little
bugs circled frantically, just above the circle
of pipe smoke —our fragile umbrella
torn too quickly by the wind.

We lay in silence
thoughts dispersed and unaimed.
Our souls wandered with the breeze
through fresh grass of May.
We joined the bee on the buttercup
and tasted wild nectar.
We drifted with clouds
fast through the sea.

We turned to a sound,
and joined a woodchuck
nibbling his lunch. Black eyes
shining, nose quivering,
jaws chewing. He ate fast, greedily.
Perhaps we wondered
in some dark subconscious recesses (for
we never thought it until later)
why the bugs did not go over and bother
him awhile. He at least had fur.

But if we wondered it, we did not think it.
Bugs bothered us, but not our nibbling friend.
One of us scratched or slapped. Our friend's
composure was lost to panic,
horror as he ran, bouncing over the tall
green to some secret dark cavern he had built.

He couldn't know we loved him
and had dined with him and even savored the
taste of green with him. Perhaps though
he did know we could not fear with him.

His fear and flight returned us to ourselves,
passing springtime high on a hillside,
far from cares, lying firm against the hard
rocky ground, our bodies caressed by grass
and breeze, our spirits by the
ocean above and the life within.

We lay and watched the spring flow past.
We were not sad, nor alone, nor empty
for when our souls ventured out we joined
their flight, looked back and saw our bodies
composed in peace on the hard and rocky hillside.

April Sometime

"Your grandfather is dead."

"What?"

"Your grandfather and grandmother are dead."

"How?" I could think of no other response.

"House burned down. They didn't get out."

"When?"

"Last night. Your Dad just called."

I sat down, dazed. I didn't know my grandfather too well. I'd heard his story, or parts of it, of course, but he was still largely a mystery. I remembered my boyhood adventures on his place, often with him as a participant in some adventure I'd find myself in the midst of. I often felt a sense of agreement with him in spirit. We were alike it seemed, in the retrospection of twenty years or so. My grandfather was a rare breed, the only one in the family who did not condemn my wanderlust. It seemed strange, that he had lived fifty years in the same house. I'd never made two. Before the end of two years, as if there were some invisible alarm clock set with an alarm I could not ignore, I moved. I never had to. I always cried as I was leaving. I never left a place I didn't love, yet there was always some other place to experience. My wife did not condemn. She shared the sense of adventure. My kids did too. But they had to. My mother claimed I was unhappy (I never thought so) my father said I was afraid to stay longer than two years because someone would get close to me, would be a friend. He said I couldn't abide anyone close to me. He was wrong too. I moved from place to place for the same reason I write or get up each morning. Adventure, curiosity, and a challenge to the fates. Now, my only aly was dead. Grandfather had once said,

"Some day beauty, time and fate will make you stop and the fever will leave you."

At thirty-seven the fever hasn't left. Now I have to go across half a continent from Minnesota to Maine for a funeral.

"Call Duluth, honey. I'll fly out now."

The old fire chief picked me up at the motel to take me out to the farm.

"What happened?" I asked the chief. He remained silent.

"What happened? Can you tell me anything?" I was insistent.

"They burned up." He stared straight ahead, driving.

"That's all? Do you know that it was they?"

He grunted. "Two bodies. Charred bad. Black long piles of ash. Nothing to identify, but it was."

They were old people past eighty. They had been active, though, and had been celebrated in the local paper last fall for their sixty-third wedding anniversary. It was Saturday. On Monday they were to have moved to Connecticut to live with Dad. They were too old to live alone. Dad had just recently convinced them to move to Connecticut.

The fire chief stared at the rubble. He poked at it with his toe. I walked around, listening to the chief muttering.

"What did you say?" I asked, not wanting to miss anything, hanging onto any thread that may make a sense of order from disaster.

"I said, _'twarnt no reason._'"

"No reason?"

"No. They weren't poor. House in perfect condition."

Arthur Winacre would never let anything be less than perfect. So why? Just before spring. Just before the snow left altogether. Why at all? Why now? The sap rising in the trees, the land lying quietly beneath his feet almost in anticipation of the burst into spring/life.

"Can you remember when he first came here?" I asked the old chief.

The chief made the sound that passed for _yes_ down east.

"Would you tell me about him? I've been sort of an outcast from my family for a long time. I've heard Dad say some things, of course, but I'd really like to know more."

"What you want to know?" The chief hesitated, distrustful.

"Whatever you will tell me. Everything. What was he like, when did he come here?"

The chief kicked the ground, reluctant, as will all his breed to talk at length on any subject.

"He was a stranger, an outsider. Bought the old Rufus Johnson place. Over 150 acres of brush, a falling down barn and a dilapidated old house. They had three children. They moved in one summer. Simply occupied the place as though it were theirs. As though the ghost of Rufus Johnson didn't exist."

There was an abrupt stop. I was about to ask about the "haunted" rumor, but he went on.

"Guess it really never was haunted. He jumped in and began to fix and paint. He re-did the outside so it looked good. Tore down the barn, built a few good small outbuildings. Made the place and about five acres around it look good. Didn't do much for the rest, though. Just let it grow however it wanted. Never prodded or cut. It took ten years for folks to start calling it the name he give it. They accepted the place, the name, but not him. He was always an outsider. But I guess he wanted it that way. He educated their kids at school, helped anyone who needed help, accepted help whenever he needed it and it was offered, did all the things a good neighbor might be expected to do. But he was different."

"How was he different?" I interrupted, taking sudden offense at the word.

"Not really different. But there was something."

"What?" I was eager for him to continue.

"I remember once he told me that _we_ were the outsiders, not him."

"How did he figure that?"

"Well." The chief looked at me, glaring a little, "he said we were all born here in this town, raised in it, and died in it with no choice in it. Like nationality or religion, he said, you're born with one. Nothing you can do will change either very much or for very long. We were here just by chance. But he wasn't. He'd selected it, adopted it. He had seen a lot of the world and this is where he chose to reside. He selected his home and because he selected he could leave, because he hadn't loved it, hadn't known of it, he could love it. He said none of us had ever done nothing, just been here. We were the outsiders.''

The old chief paused, winded from talking. As we slowly walked back towards the car, I thought how lucky he had been to find a home and stay in it forever. I had had a home once. Dad sold it. It wasn't very fancy, but it was picturesque and I lived in it until I went into the Air Force. When I returned three years later, Dad had sold it. Had to I guess. He and Mom had built a new little modern house not far from there. All the walls were fresh and straight. The floors were all level and it was awfully little. Like a small brick hospital or something. I lived there a few weeks and then left to seek some fortune or wife or something. Since then I had been on tour and nothing yet had stopped me. Now I was at my grandfather's place, the place where my father had been raised and had lived as a boy and it was burned to the ground and I felt sorry for my father. The chief interrupted my thoughts,

"I don't know as many people agreed with him, or even understood him, though the words were clear enough all right. But the town never did accept him.''

"But he was always here. For nearly fifty years he's been here. Came as a young man with a young family. Grew them up right, until the war that he wouldn't let them boys go to took the oldest one too hard-headed to go over into Canada like he told him to. Was only eighteen. Body came back and was buried there on the place. He made it official and made it a family graveyard, with one grave. People around came to offer condolances for two or three days, bringing food and sending flowers until Arthur got suddenly angry. He cussed us like only an educated man with a feeling for the language can cuss and wouldn't allow no one at the burial. It was just he and his family and the undertaker.'' He paused as though to catch his breath.

"Rumor had it that he wouldn't even let them cover the coffin. He cussed them all away and did it himself. A year later his daughter died in bed of some illness that was never made public. It was the same thing. Only he didn't let it go for two or three days. He ran everyone out after one. There was just one left. Sixteen he was when they left. Didn't sell the place, or rent it. Just boarded it up and drove off. Three years later, when they stopped fighting they came back. As if nothing had happened. He was teaching again and working the place enough, I guess, for food. He fished a good bit, taught school and minded his own business. His boy —your Dad— went away to school, had planned to be a doctor, I heard. Arthur was still separated from us by the wall he had built years ago and reinforced twice. But he seemed happy. He liked that wall. He was a good neighbor. He kept the place up, and enjoyed life and friends. The friends always on his terms of course.''

"All of this makes him different, or strange?" I asked. I didn't say I thought I understood.

He ignored my tone. "I don't know what it was," the chief went on, "but when I'd see him working the big berry patch, or tending his chickens, or taking care of some of the chores I got the feeling I was seeing something unusual. Sometimes he'd be so engrossed in whatever he was doing, or thinking —he never was doing very much, really— he wouldn't even hear me until I yelled. Then he'd say, "I'm sorry I didn't hear you. I was listening to the morning come." Or, "I was watching the dirt glisten in the sun." Or, "Yea, it is a nice day."

"Nice day? It could be bleak and dreary with icy rain spitting against your face. Maybe the last rain of the year, whipping the last leaves, or maybe just a damp cold November drizzle that don't do nothing but promise to freeze you later, while it is freezing you at 42 degrees instead of at 32 and he'd say it was *nice.*"

"Great weather to be out in, to watch and feel. Makes a man feel like a man. Lets him know how it is to be little, insignificant, let's him know what God is, even where he is."

The road curved gently as we headed back toward town. The old chief went on, warmed to the tale, forgetting he was a taciturn, stern old downeaster.

"He talked about God like that a lot, but my old preacher said he was atheist heathen. Wouldn't believe in Jesus or nothing. Cussed him out and chased him off once soon after he got here. Actually threatened to shoot him if he read or tried to read anything over the graves he filled up himself. Preacher said he'd offered to pray for him and he said, *You pray for me and I'll see you in hell.* Never could figure that one out. He was not just making words, he meant exactly what he said, the preacher said.

I asked him once how he came to pick this almost isolated little New England village.''

I could hear my grandfather telling me the answer as he had many years before. His voice was clear in my memory,

"I picked it for a lot of reasons. Partly because it is almost isolated. Partly because it is beautiful, and because the seasons here are so dramatic. It is a good place to raise a family and to have a home that you searched for for fifteen years. I guess really any place that had beauty —as I get older I'm convinced Keats was right—''

"Who?" I interrupted.

"John Keats, a poet.''

"Oh.'' I didn't know anything about poets then, but I learned and was coming to agree with Keats and grandpa.

"that I happened to be in when I said I want to stop would have been all right. I was here. I bought this place with no intention of staying. Then I began to work on it and got it how I like it and suddenly I didn't own it anymore. It owned me. The day I realized that I was home. Like being married when you're in love with your wife. One day, driving up the highway you realize how completely you are owned by her, possessed by her. She possesses you in love. It is her house. No matter what you do to a house, if there's a woman in it it is hers. She feeds you, loves you and finally you are owned. You realize it and say, Yes, isn't it great! When it owns you, you are home.''

The chief's voice interrupted my memory. He was saying, "Your grandpa said that this place didn't belong to him. It belonged to Rufus Johnson, and his fathers, or maybe the first man that ever walked on it. He said that you can't own anything you care about. As soon as you begin to care, it owns you.''

The chief stopped in front of my motel and I walked slowly back to the road. No place owns me. Not yet. Hadn't grandpa said he searched for fifteen years? Well, that's about as long as I had been at it. Now I am stuck out in Minnesota. Beautiful? Yes, sort of. Did I like my home? Yes it was nice. Did it own me? No. I'd lived there two years and all I could think about was (not leaving) going to some other place.

Grandpa's dead now. He and grandma. They were young for the

eighties. They were going to leave here, to sell it. Now they won't. I've got an idea he didn't want or even intend to go anyway. He once told me he'd never leave this place. That his will was all fixed to be buried by his children. He said the place was his son's, who didn't need it or want it, but who had children, one of which might, and he said the place would "use them good."

The funeral services were quiet. Dad had them conducted a c c o r d -
ing to his father's will. Buried beside their children, accepted by the land, if not by the people that lived nearby on it. It was the day after the burial that Dad and I got a chance to talk.

"Did they find out why it burned?" I asked.

"No."

"He was clever."

"What?"

"He did it."

"Did what?"

"Burned the place, himself and grandmother in it."

"How do you know?"

"I just know. He told me he could never sell it or leave it. Said he belonged here, the place owned them free and clear, no mortgage left to foreclose. It was too late."

"No. He agreed to move in with me. They both did."

"You tried to force him. To shut you up he agreed. But he —no, not him alone, they— they, the two of them, planned this. They'd rather die here than live somewhere else."

"But why?" Dad asked, fishing for straws, "Can you prove it?"

"No. He'd never give us the satisfaction of knowing. He was eighty-four, but still sharp enough, clever enough."

"I guess he was." Dad said slowly. Then, "And how is it with my vagabond son, are you content in Minnesota?"

"Content? What's content?"

"I mean are you going to stay there? Stay put for once in your life? God if you'd just stay in one place more than two years. Any place. All this moving around isn't good for you or the kids. Look at how much it costs."

"I don't know about Minnesota. It's not the East, that's for sure."

"You have to move out there, 2,000 miles from your mother and me, so we don't even get the pleasure of our grandchildren. I suppose next you'll be needing to borrow some money to move farther west.?"

"No. I don't think so. But I did read that they are desperate for teachers in Nigeria." My father winced in pain. The contours of his face seemed to be the contours of a hill just in front of my grandfather's house.

Of Time, The Boy, And The River

The bass had been popping like popcorn all over the broad, fast mountain river. They leaped high, clearing the water by a foot and more as they tried to catch the hovering dragonfly.

He had arrived early that Friday to the camp he was growing up in. A budding angler and a budding man, seeking without realization, the truth of wildness, the truths of the river; truths never articulated, but truths lived.

He was alone. He had come early, ahead of family and friends who filled the weekend with joy and motion and noise not always welcome. All that spring he had been working at learning what the river and her game had to teach. He had waded the ledges and riffles, catching bass and bluegills and an occasional catfish on natural baits; helgramites, nitecrawlers, and minnows. His catches had been small in size and number, but he was not really aware of that. Each catch was more lesson than fish. A lesson he had to master, its mastery its own reward. The old man who lived alone in the old farm house where the camp was, had told him that he would become a good fisherman when he became one with the river. When the passage of time on the river was subconsciously unrecorded.

He did not understand the old man's ideas. At least not always, and never completely. He liked to talk with him and considered him wise. They always talked when he arrived for the weekend's fishing. The old man had promised to show him where he could get his deer. But this weekend he was concerned with bass.

During the week before he had read an article on *multiple spinners and flies for trout*. The article had dealt with New England trout and trolling in small ponds. The idea of many spinners did not, somehow, appeal to him. But spinners? Yes. They were small and he had begun to feel that most of the lures he had were too large for most of the fish in the river.

He had spent some of his little money on silver and gold spinners, double-bladed and single. On a hunch, he had bought a jar of small thin pork rind strips. He had flies, blotched up messes of feather and tinsel he had tied himself. Not pretty, but they had always caught fish.

Now in the late afternoon sun, standing beside his old 1935 Chevy coupe, he was rigging his spinning tackle. He selected a double-bladed silver spinner, a fairly large black gnat and a thin strip of pork about an inch-and-a-half long. He did not go near the cabin, but walked down to the crystal clear water and flipped the lure ten feet out to check the spin of the blades. It looked good, but he instantly realized that he would need more weight. He clipped on a sinker a foot ahead of the lure and looped the line so the sinker would not slip down against the lure. He flipped it out again and watched. The same. He knew that it was good. He checked his pockets for the plastic boxes and stepped into the summercool river.

He fished slowly and carefully and was rewarded with occasional big bluegills and small bass that had to be returned. The legal minimum size was ten inches. Most of the ones he caught were eight to nine.

He worked upriver about a quarter of a mile, working the ledges that he knew held fish, good fish. He had four nice bluegills hanging from his belt when he saw a bass boil the water near the bank. The bass was near a weeping willow whose boughs hung into the water. The water roiled over his rise as it would for a very large fish, so he had started working that way, slowly.

As he came into casting range he examined the hole. A gentle current was tugging at his legs, but between where he was standing and the bank, the water was flat and still. The willow was reflected and doubled in the clear water. There was a log, ghostly white, angling downstream on the water, originating beneath the spring bows of the willow. The hole was perhaps twenty feet long and water appeared to be about waist deep. The bank was a good cast away. He thought of the pictures he had seen in magazines. Here was one that belonged there. But the picture he experienced was not printable. It included the billowing clouds, the eagle soaring on high thermal currents, the warm sun on his back and the cool water gently tugging at the lower half of his body. There was silence, with a magical majesty, as though the earth waited. It may also have been a magic moment in youth, one that is at once past and yet never past, always as part of the man. A part that would last beyond his three-score-and-ten, even forever.

The gentle plop of the lure hitting the water on the outer edge of the hole did not even disturb the silence. It was a gently hollow, almost distant sound within the inverted bowl that was his world.

The strike was instant, and a ten-inch bass was soon finning beside him. Good for the stringer. He cast again. Another. This one exploded across the surface, rupturing the silence. This one was twelve inches long. He smiled and carefully strung the fish through both lips. He cast again and played the fish. Nearly every cast produced a strike and he thrilled at the pulsating power and wild acrobatics of the bronzed warriors. He did not move his feet, but worked all the hole. His forty-second bass filled his limit of eight. They were all between ten and twelve inches. The big one he had come for either did not exist, or would wait for another day. To many, and perhaps even to himself, his catch was nothing spectacular, but as he carefully strung his limit catch, afternoon was passing into evening and the purple twilight added to the scene. It was his first limit.

As he debated releasing the last fish a car horn sounded three times. Family had arrived. Color was beginning to fade, the billowing while clouds faded from the surface of the water. A crow cawed off to his left, another answered. He shook his head in disbelief. Three hours had passed without measurement. Time had stood still. For an instant he had held eternity in his grasp, experienced it. Now the car horn, and perhaps the crow, signalled that it was over, lost forever in the ghost that is the past. He looked down at his eight bass, finning lazily in the light current on his downstream side. Quickly he reached down and released them one by one and watched them swim away into the darkening river.

He could not have told anyone why he released those eight beautiful smallmouths. He tried at camp, but only his mother had seemed to understand. He could not understand why it made her cry.

The Rites Of Spring

Though it was the moon of melting and thawing, it was snowing. The snow/sleet stung his face as he sat on the bank of the river. It was a big river. Not the biggest he had seen, but big. It was fast and tumbling its ice chips into water that lay still and deepened and lessened twice each day.

His language had a word for it, but his language is lost to us. His tribe, maybe even his race, is lost with the word. We know he was there, had always been there, just as I, as modern man was there, seeking surcease of winter. I know what he felt on that very late February day we shared through eons. We shared impatience. Impatience We both would feel through the forever days of March as we searched for April when the dogwood burst and the shad found the river. It is for me as it was for him. We, that man of 500 and 5,000 and numbers larg and meaningless, years ago, and I share through time the rites of spring on the Rappahanock. The time when the shad come back to spawn. This is our story. His and mine, and yours, if you've ever longed for spring and the surge of a powerful fish against your rod. With the Indians it may have been a gathering, a time for feasting, for saving. For me it is a religious experience, deep and eternal and vital. His life was more in tune with the natural rhythm of the earth than mine is. I know that for him too, it was more than food.

The winter had been long, cold and the snows deep. The strong of his people had survived, the weak, the old, had gone into the c o l d -
ness and could not return. The tribe would live on, growing in the

bellies of the women, the lifegivers. But he was hungry now, and it was time for the fish to come back to the river. It was almost the moon of the growing grass when all the earth awakens. When the sun would warm flesh that was too long cold and dry.

He had never heard of Persephone or Demeter. But I had, and I knew it was time. Time for Persephone to come from the underworld and for Demeter to rejoice. Time for the Virginia nights to be soft and warm again. It was not that time. It was almost that time. I, just as he, stood on the banks in mid March and stared deeply into the swollen river to see if the fish were back. It was too early. I knew that. But I was there, so I flipped my baited hook into the muddy water anyway. Instantly I caught a white perch. Not bad. The white perch, at least, were in. I wondered what name he would have given to them.

It was the time when the small white stick-back fish came in from the water that rose and fell twice each day. That was good. That meant the slender, long white fish would soon find the river. He would be able to see them, hundreds of them, coming up the first riffle above the flat water. His people would begin now to make the nets and traps and baskets that they would use during the greening moon. He would report to the tribe. He turned and left the river with news for his people.
"The fish are back."

The first fish of spring is always cause for celebration. It signals the end of a long winter when the weather has kept me indoors watching football games and the *The American Sportsman.*

While not a rite of spring, that first fish is a symbol, a promise. The rites will begin soon now. The six-inch white perch is proof. Regardless of what the calendar said, soon it would be spring. Not on March 21, but on some mid-April weekend when the shad hit the dart again and bend the rod and tire the arm, when I stand in the icy river with water to my crotch and my son beside me, both with bowed rods and seventeen inches of shad tailwalking across the rapids, when I can look over and smile and think of the *Old Milwaukee* commercial and mean it when I say,

''Son, it doesn't get any better than this.''

His tribe began to chatter with excitement at the news. The women began to build and repair nets, the men began to weave and build traps. Young braves built many spears, and the youngest got their hide-and-bone catchers made new. The chief and the shamman chanted prayers to the great spirit and the **spiritus mundi** *that would come to life in green. The great white fish would soon be here and there would be great feasting and joy and the great spirits would be thanked and there would be chants and dancing and more feasting. All the tribe knew it was time, but until he, or some other brave, saw the first fish, the time was not yet. Now the time is and they have waited for it through long snows and winds when the ground turned all to stone and the creeks did not run and they waited, and they buried their dead and still they knew it would come and it had come and they were all re-born. The celebration would last most of the moon of greening.*

The river is alive in April as in no other time. It is full of fish, the banks and rocks are full of fishermen, mostly dipping or netting herring. Families come down and picnic, canoes and kayacks challenge the white water, there are camp fires and roasting hot dogs, coffee, and beer for later when the afternoon warms. There are kids fishing with worms for the white perch, wives and girlfriends trying not to look too bored as their man fishes in whichever way suits him. There are lines of spin-fishermen casting tiny darts and spinners and spoons to a fish that does not feed while in fresh water. The osprey dives, there is a spalsh and he lifts himself laboriously with a foot-long herring wriggling in his talons. Cars zip by above on the US 1 bridge. It is a strange mixture, but here I am alone in a sea of humanity, almost oblivious to the world's intrusion and boistrous presence. I know that he who stood here 500, 5,000 or more years ago had no such intrusions. He prob ably caught three-foot white shad, while I must settle for hickory shad from fourteen to nineteen inches.

His future is me. I am his heir. The product of the process, of progress, of evolution, of technology, of fear and terror and war and peace and doubt and death and birth and birth again. Five hundred, five thousand, coutless more years separate us, but in the dive of the osprey from a blue sky on a hot afternoon in late April,we are not separated at all. We are one and time has stood still and it is forever.

shanti, shanti, shanti

The Conservatory Of American Letters is a non-profit Maine Corporation dedicated to discovering, publishing, promoting and encouraging literary talent. C.A.L. believes that much good to great literature is being lost because of the economics of commercial publishing.

C.A.L. invites anyone who reads, writes, or admires literary art to get involved. Send a self-addressed stamped (.22) envelope for information.

Conservatory Of American Letters
PO Box 123
South Thomaston, Maine 04858